It's Ok Not To Cry

Gina Schampers

BALBOA.
PRESS
A DIVISION OF HAY HOUSE

Balboa Press books may be ordered through booksellers or by contacting:

Balboa Press
A Division of Hay House
1663 Liberty Drive
Bloomington, IN 47403
www.balboapress.com
1 (877) 407-4847

Because of the dynamic nature of the Internet, any web addresses or links contained in this book may have changed since publication and may no longer be valid. The views expressed in this work are solely those of the author and do not necessarily reflect the views of the publisher, and the publisher hereby disclaims any responsibility for them.

The author of this book does not dispense medical advice or prescribe the use of any technique as a form of treatment for physical, emotional, or medical problems without the advice of a physician, either directly or indirectly. The intent of the author is only to offer information of a general nature to help you in your quest for emotional and spiritual well-being. In the event you use any of the information in this book for yourself, which is your constitutional right, the author and the publisher assume no responsibility for your actions.

Any people depicted in stock imagery provided by Thinkstock are models, and such images are being used for illustrative purposes only.
Certain stock imagery © Thinkstock.

Print information available on the last page.

ISBN: 978-1-5043-5091-4 (sc)
ISBN: 978-1-5043-5092-1 (e)

Balboa Press rev. date: 2/19/2016

Contents

Acknowledgements

I would like to thank everyone who sent our family condolences, love and support during difficult times.

Dedications

This book is dedicated to my parents who have passed, and my sisters who have always been there for me at any point in my life. It is also dedicated to my fiancé, who is the most amazing person, father, and partner in life. I could not have done this without all of you! Love you!

Chapter 1

Introduction

My intention for this book is to help others who have gone through a loss. If you can get one thing out of this book then I have succeeded, and you are one step closer to healing. One of my sisters explained to me that reading this book like going through grief. It tends to read like a roller coaster, much like how grief is. She said she was laughing one minute, then tears, and back to laughing. I hope it brings some smiles to you and really hope that *It's Ok Not to Cry* is able to help you in some way!

Life is never the same, from that moment you hear any bad news. The news could be that someone is sick, has cancer or that someone passed away unexpectedly. Your thoughts change, your views and outlook on life and death change. Your memories of a person start to surface. Your life is drastically impacted because of this incident. You realize you took for granted a lot of things; peace and bliss that things were ok. You took for granted having that person in your life, health, or companionship. Once it happens to you and affects your life, you would never wish what you went through on your worse enemies. It is life altering!

I always thought about writing a book to talk about my story so it could maybe in some way help people get through a difficult time. I always loved this quote, **"To know even one life has breathed easier because you have lived. This is to have succeeded." –Ralph Waldo Emerson.** I have had the need to write down my story in hopes of helping others. I still remember watching the movie, *The Shift,* with Wayne Dyer and he kept saying, **"Don't die with your music still in you"**. It took me awhile to understand what he meant by that, until I remembered a book I started writing which would turn into a version of this one. After losing my original draft, I recognized I should start writing again. I do not claim to be an expert on death, dying or the grieving process, this is just my story and what I went through. I have lost a great grandma, one aunt, one uncle, both grandmas and both parents by the age of 28.

I believe there is no one right way to grieve, everyone goes through it differently. Nobody can tell you how to grieve. What I have found was reading relatable stories and hearing similar situations to find out how they got through it. I liked finding out that they were able to be alright. I also liked to see that there is hope to be happy one day, or that someday maybe I will get out of this funk and live life in my "new normal". Life would never be the same, but learning how to live my "new normal" was a task I was searching for. **"This is a thing many people outside your grief cannot understand: that you have not simply lost one person, at one point in time. You have lost their presence in every aspect of your life. Your future has changed as well as your "now.""** -Megan Devine. You learn to live without them here and that unfortunately becomes your new normal.

It sounds painful and a task you do not want to do, but it is the reality I was faced with. Like most, I had to go with the situation that was presented to me. Often times I wondered if what I was feeling and doing was normal for a person in my situation. I wondered if my sisters and I laughed our way through both our parents funerals and I was not crying that much, was that OK? Or was I doing what I was supposed to be doing to grieve? That was the basis for the title of the book. Just because you are not crying over a death of a loved one does not mean that is wrong. It is ok not to cry!

It's Ok Not to Cry is divided up by people and categories. When I would seek out grief books or stories online, I would always search to find people similar to me. Looking for stories on people who have lost a father, or a few years later I was searching for how younger people coped with being an "adult orphan". How did other people deal with the fact that they do not have any parents anymore? Or how did a young person, specifically, deal with that same situation? I wanted to know that what I was feeling was common and not so crazy. In a way I wanted to justify my feelings, but also somehow find comfort in knowing I am not the only one in this situation. **"Don't allow others to rush your grief. You have a lifetime to heal and it's a lifelong journey, travel at your own speed!" – The Greif Tool Box**

Chapter 2

My Dad

"My father gave me the greatest gift anyone could give another person, he believed in me." – Jim Valvano

My dad always had some piece of advice for his daughters. He used to say, "Two in the bush is worth more than one in the hand". I never really knew what he meant, come to find out that is not the actual saying! Besides his mixed up sayings, he was a wise man that I always looked up to. My dad was a jack of all trades. There wasn't anything he could not do or fix. He would build house, duplexs, and decks in the summer months when he was not teaching math in our High School.

I loved hanging out the garage with him when he was building things. You could say I was a daddy's girl! I loved going to the grocery store with him- not to ask for anything, but just to go with him. My dad was the first one I would go to ask a question on something, even when I was in college. In my college years his advice changed a bit to saying like, "You can wish in one hand and shit in the other". That I understood!

Even after both of my parents are gone, I still find myself wasting energy on wishing they both could come back and be here physically with us again. Even a few years after my dad passed away I would still reach for the phone to call him and ask him questions. It would take me a second to remember he would not be on the other end to answer it.

I always felt that my dad was the only one who <u>really</u> understood me in my family. So when he passed away it was devastating that he was gone. It made me feel more alone than ever. I always sought to get my dad's approval on everything; I always wanted to make him proud. He was not one to come out and tell you he was proud of you for every little thing, just on the big accomplishments. So when you heard him say something that sounded like an approval, or a "not too shabby" you knew he really meant it. He was our secret cheerleaders in our success in life. Our dad was not one to really express his feelings, but you knew when he was proud of you even if he never exactly came out and said it.

I walked in the ceremony at my graduation for my Bachelor's Degree and he was there for that. They hand you an empty case that will hold your diploma, not the actual diploma, they mail that to your home address. I remember him telling me that he will believe it and will give me a graduation present when he sees that actual diploma. Well he never did. He passed away three months later.

I think my decision to go on to get my Master's Degree was a real push to do well to prove to myself that I could do it. Also, it was to show my dad that I could graduate again with him watching. That graduation day was bittersweet. My fiancé and one sister drove 400+ miles to attend it. I hoped my dad was proud of me and was a little teary when walking across the stage because he wasn't there to see it. I know now that he was there in spirit, but I wished he could have been there physically.

EVERY day before I left school as a kid my dad would say, "do your best!" He was a teacher and that might have been a part of it, but it hit home to me to do well in school. I try to take that advice into my life now when dealing with grief and processing the loss of a loved one. You do not have go through life like how some book tells you to grieve, just do your best to get through a day. If that sounds like too much, do your best to get through an hour, or a few minutes and think back on how far you have come. Celebrate those milestones and accomplishments! You made it through that phone call, funeral, burial, that first trip out of your house by yourself in public where you would see people you knew.

My mom avoided the local grocery store for almost a year after my dad passed away. She would drive an hour round-trip to go get groceries, just so she didn't have to run into people. She knew people would ask how she was doing or want to talk about our dad. It is understandable, that is sad, and you do not want to breakdown crying in public. Somethings just take time and baby steps, just celebrate the little victories in your new journey.

Phone Call

I was living across the state when I received those phone calls I will never forget. I know exactly where I was standing. I remember dropping to my knees and sobbing. I remember all the events that happened the rest of that night. I remember having amazing friends who drove me back home that next day. So many little details that I could probably not tell you about a day a month ago, but that day I will never forget! **"I never got to say goodbye. Wish I could go back to the day when angels came and took you away. I wanted** to hold your hand so tight, kiss you gently and say good night. And then just before you had to go I would tell you how much 'I love you so'. I don't know how I don't know why I never got the change to say goodbye." –John F Connor.

I was not there when my father passed away, but my sisters and my mom were. That is one thing that still gets me a little bit and I know I need to let it go. There are a few things that go with not being there; guilt, frustration, unfair feelings, sadness of time lost, sadness of that final goodbye and closure I guess. At the time I did not realize that not being there was also making me sad. Feelings were hard to put your finger on because there were so many emotions happening that were new.

I remember getting to my parent's house and nobody was there, everything just seemed so quiet and empty. My dad's rocking chair that he sat in everyday was empty. His shoes were there, but he was not. His coat was there, but he was not. His truck was there, but he was not. After about a half an hour my sisters and my mom showed up at the house. We cried, we talked, and at some point we laughed.

A few big things stand out from my dad's funeral, but one that I still think about is after the burial at the lunch. I was standing next to my mom talking to her and she paused. I asked her what was wrong or what she was doing. She said, "Wow, I just scanned the crowd looking for your father". Something she did out of habit everyday of her life, something she would not do again until she met him in heaven.

Help From a Friend

I was trying to stay afloat in life after my dad passed away. One of my friends was dating a guy we will call Jake, who I happened to work with. My friend told me to talk to Jake sometime because he also had a father pass away. I do remember sitting in the basement of the bar we worked at after our shift was over. I distinctly remember him saying, "it will get better with time, life gets easier with time, just give it some time". So when I was thinking about writing this book and including other people's stories, I felt that it was important to reach out to him. Thank you Jake for opening up about your unfortunate passing and giving me advice at that time, it really helped me. During those months I was in a dark place. Eventually I decided to seek professional help and found out I was suffering from Major Depression.

A week ago I reached out to him and asked if he would like to answer a few questions for *It's Ok Not to Cry* and here was his response:

1. What was the hardest thing for you after the loss of your loved one?

I think out of all questions this was the toughest one to answer. Trying to pick one thing out of the sea of changes that happened inside me after I lost my father is kind of difficult. I felt guilt, irrational guilt of course, but it was still there. The loss, missing my father, knowing I'll never get another word of advice or chided for the silly things I did. Then of course knowing he would miss the important things in my life, like getting married or meeting my first child. All of that was very hard for me to deal with. I would say the worst, or hardest thing was the question...why? Why take a healthy, active, happy man? Why my father? Why then? He was supposed to die an old man. I couldn't answer that one simple question. Why? Since I couldn't find an answer, I rebelled. Hated. I hated God, the universe, myself, because nobody could answer that one simple question. That is what tore me up the most.

2. What advice would you give someone who is grieving?

Keep moving. Life doesn't stop after tragedy, and the people we lost wouldn't want us to fall behind. Getting up, and pushing through the numbness, the pain, the depression, creates a routine. It's the routine that carries you, sometimes on auto-pilot in those later months when the grief comes back around. After enough time, when the wound does start to heal, and it does start to heal, you will look back and be thankful you kept moving, it will feel like strength, and that strength will then help you deal with the next tragedy.

3. What helped you most in your grieving process?

This is another question that is hard to boil down to one answer. I took from so many things to help me along my way to healing. My friends reminded me I wasn't alone, my family reminded me I was loved, and art helped me express my feelings, even if only to myself in a healthy way. All of that was important, but I think the one thing that stands out the most, was forgiveness. I forgave "God" or the universe, whatever it was that I blamed for taking my father away from me without giving me a reason. I forgave myself for how I felt. But in the end it's always time. Time helps the most, but it's also the most difficult thing to understand, or explain to someone.

About six years later this is still his advice, give it time. You do not really understand that when you are in the thick of it, but take if from a few people who have gone through a tragic loss that time does help heal. It doesn't mean you will be 100% better. It does mean you can get through life without breaking down and crying every few minutes or having those terrible feelings all the time. There is hope and after a little bit of time those feelings will subside and happiness will return to you.

Chapter 3

My Mom

That Day

Ring…ring…ring… one phone call can change your life forever. You go through life doing the same routine day after day, until that one day when your world is turned upside down. Those moments in life make you wish you were a kid again when a book on your mom's lap made everything better. The days of saying, "Mommy, I need your help" are over.

The decision to answer my cell phone when I was just getting into work will never escape my mind. Our work policy is no personal calls during work hours or use of your cell phone, but when you see your oldest sister calling you at 7:15am you know you should answer. I answered the phone, "Hello? What's up?"

My sister responded, "Hi, are you at work?"

"Yeah, what's going on?" I said.

"Are you by people? Are you sitting down?" she said.

"Your scaring me, what is going on?" I said.

"I just got a call from the police department, they found mom lying on the street and took her to the hospital in an ambulance and it doesn't look good." She said with a tremble in her voice.

"You kidding me, right? NO!" I said as I started to sob and finally sit down.

She proceeded to talk on the phone telling me some details about how the neighbors tried to get ahold of me, but so many thoughts kept running through my head. I need to leave, I need to tell my boss I am leaving, I need to call my boyfriend, when finally I heard my name loudly in the phone.

"Yeah?" I said.

"You need to call Mike, please promise me you will call him? Are you OK to drive yourself?" she said.

"I will and yeah, I will be fine!" I said.

After talking quickly to my boss, I left. I still remember calling him breaking down crying on the way out of the building as the black automatic doors slid open. I kept telling everyone I was fine to drive, in reality that drive was one big haze. He met me at his dad's house where we were staying at the time, because we were in the middle of building our house. He drove us to the hospital and we met all my sisters and brother-in-law there.

These are the details we found out; it all started on the Monday after 4th of July weekend. My mother went for a walk that morning after church. She did not have her ID on her, just her car keys. She passed out, out of nowhere due to a bleed in her brain (not an aneurism). We were told these things just happen sometimes even to healthy people, which she was! The owner of the house came out and called 911, the police came to the scene performed CPR and was able to revive her breathing.

We still believe her soul had left her body that morning before the paramedics showed up. We believe the only reason why they were able to revive her, was because she was an organ donor.

Since the oxygen supply was cut off from the brain for so long she started to swell up in the face and was unrecognizable. The police took a photo of her that they took on scene and brought it around town. They brought the photo to churches, businesses, and people's homes, all places of which she had volunteered on a regular basis and normally would have been recognizable. She stayed 24 hours in the hospital as 'Jane Doe'.

The police department was able to identify her because she had her car keys on her. They went into the system, pulled up what type of vehicle the keys belonged to. Then the police cross referenced that with owners of that vehicle in our small town of 3,000 people. The police then walked up to those houses and used the clicker to hear if it opened the doors of the vehicle. They talked to the neighbors that Tuesday morning when they finally found the car. That is when they called my sister, and my phone rang…ring…ring…ring. "Hello? What's up?" I said.

When your 28 years old, 6 months pregnant with your first child, and your father had passed away five years ago, you do not expect to get a phone call saying your healthy mother (who walks 5-10 miles a day, swims weekly and volunteers for everything under the sun) has now been taken from your life, and you will never be able to say anything to her again. Cherish those moments you have with your parents, as life can take them away so unexpectedly, with just one phone call!

Days Following

When Mike and I walked into the hospital to find my sisters, it was one of those numbing "Holy shit" moments! The reality finally hit me that this was real and the situation was not good. My prego self-walked into that tiny hospital room with a body lying in a bed, it wasn't my mom. It was her physical body, but she was not there, we could all sense it. She did not look like herself, her hair was all mangled, and that was not my mom. She always had to comb or "pick" her hair, as she would say, before she left the house. She always carried a pick in her purse to fix her hair before she got out the car or in a public bathroom if we went anywhere.

Her face was all swollen from the lack of oxygen when she collapsed. They had her on a breathing machine with a tube just hanging out of her mouth. You could see her chest going up and down mechanically. That noise... I will never in my life ever forget that noise of the breathing machine. Anytime I have been in a hospital since then it feels like my heart skips a beat when I hear breathing machines coming from someone's room. Ick, I don't even like thinking about it! I just got goose bumps writing that and thinking about it again. I think it is a memory trigger for me, because we heard it for a week straight and there were so many emotions tied to that noise. It was the only constant thing from that whole week. It was a roller coaster of emotions and events that is for sure.

The only reason she was kept on the machines to keep her alive was because she was an organ donor. We had to decide if the doctors should do the test to see if there is any brain activity, if there was not then we had to talk next steps of organ donation. If there was then we had to make some decisions they told us. All four of us knew there was not going to be any brain activity; it didn't even cross my mind that she was there mentally. Like I mentioned before we all felt that her soul left her body when she collapsed. The only reason we think that the paramedics were able to revive her and get her on a machine, was because she was meant to donate her organs. She did eventually get to donate her tissue and one organ on day four of the hospital experience.

The Funeral

That day seemed all too familiar; I had gone through this once before with my father's funeral. Now I was in the same church again looking down the aisle at the same type of casket. I wanted to speak at my mom's funeral I am not sure why, but I really felt the need to say something. I still have the paper somewhere, but I do remember saying, **"It is not the length of life, but the depth." Ralph Waldo Emerson.** My mom really touched a lot of people's lives in her years on this earth. I find myself thinking "what would my mom do in this situation?" A lot of my answers tend to be to just have faith that it will all work out.

A story I told at my mom's funeral makes me laugh now, even though at the time I was so frustrated and angry. I rode with her to one of my nephew's basketball tournaments in a town about 20 miles away. We get to the town and I asked if she knew which school it was at, and she told me no.

So I asked her, "Do you know where you are going?"

"No," she said, without any worry in her voice.

She got off the highway and just kept driving. Meanwhile I am texting my sister to find out where we are supposed to be going. I asked her how she is going to know where we have to go. This was her response:

"Oh, I'll just follow this car they are probably going to the same place." She said.

This is a town of about 73,000 people with a major interstate that runs through it. I just could not fathom how she was so calm. I didn't understand how she thought that this one car (out of all the cars passing through) is going to be going to the same Elementary School basketball tournament that we were. So we followed the car for a few minutes, as I am trying to call my sister and anyone else at this point, the car in front of us turns into a driveway to a house.

"Oh... I guess they aren't going to the tournament like I thought." My mom said matter of factly.

So after about four wrong stops and four different schools we finally arrived a half hour late. My sister told me I was so mad I wouldn't even talk. I don't really remember that part, but the next time we went to a tournament together that was the big joke- that my mom can't drive or we won't get there until it is over. I laugh at it now, because it is funny looking back at how fine my mother was with just leaving it up to faith to get there. Not sure I would have done the same thing, but that is just who she was.

She was the type of person who tried to leave her cares and worries up to someone else. My mom focused her energy on other things like helping people. If something didn't go her way, her response was, "Well, I guess I wasn't supposed to do that," or, "I guess better things are supposed to come for me." And she would just leave it at that and move on. I commend her for being like that! Sometimes I find myself worrying and have to remind myself how my mother would react and just move on. I miss a lot about her every day, but her advice is a big one I miss.

The "Why?"

I still have not really understood why both of my parents had to pass away. I think I am still trying to grasp that concept. I think that "why" might always be a question to me. My questioning of the situation is not in a sorrowful way, I have accepted the death of both of my parents, but more of a curiosity. Why did this have to happen to us in this lifetime? What are we supposed to learn from it? Why was it my sisters and I the ones to have to go through this pain and at the times that they did? Like Jake, I fixated on the "why" for a very long time and I think that is where some of my anger of the situation came from.

So many others have lost both parents. We are not the first and definitely will not be the last, but why us? What was it supposed to teach each one of us? **"When you come out of the storm you won't be the same person that walked in. That's what the storm is all about." -Haruki Murakami.** Part of me thinks that it was supposed to happen to each of us maybe to change us for the better. Maybe the situation was supposed to happen to help us appreciate each other more? I am not sure at this point, it is a concept that I continue to explore. I hope that one day I will gain a little bit of closure on that part.

Chapter 4

Grandparents

**"Grandmothers create memories that the
heart holds forever."
-Unknown**

Losing a grandparent is terrible in many ways. I was younger when I lost my first grandma. I was in 6th grade and it was my first real understanding of a funeral and death. I understood to a point that I would not see her again, but it was not life altering for me at the time. I remember other people being super sad, having to shop for funeral clothes, and cleaning out the house with my aunts and uncles. I also remember my mom bought us all a piece of jewelry to remember her, but otherwise I do not remember much. That is pretty sad looking back that it did not affect me more than that. I guess I do not have a ton of memories of her compared to my other grandmother who I spent more years with though.

When she was sick I remember being mad and not understanding why my parents would not let me go see my grandma. From what I remember they told me her lungs were filling up with fluids and she did not look like herself. That was the reason why they did not want me to see her. At the time I was mad because others got to go, but I did not. Looking back now I am very thankful they did not let me! I never had that picture in my mind of what she looked like when she was sick and in those last days.

I have a memory of her when she was laughing playing cards at her Christmas party. Other memories of her were wearing a giant straw hat in her garden. She taught me what potato bugs were. I remember summers holding an ice cream pail with water, picking potato bugs off of the plants. In the spring time she always wore one of those plastic bags (that's what I thought it was when I was younger) over her permed hair when it rained. In the winter my grandma would always have a Kleenex shoved in her sleeve just in case. It was those little things I will remember of her now.

There was one Christmas carolers came to her house when we were there. For years I thought she gave them a loaf of bread when they left! Come to find out that she used to bake cookies (amazing molasses cookies) and store them in bread bags. So apparently she gave the carolers a bag of cookies instead of bread! She was my mother's mom so it only makes sense now that she was so giving and a wonderful woman!

My other grandma died a few months before my dad and that was very hard for me. It was probably the first big death that I experienced for someone close to me. She was a super funny, goofy lady who had those sayings like "crumps", "cotton pickin'", "davenport", "arse hole", "crumps 'o Friday", those words that you giggle at when you hear older people say. She was super talented at crocheting, and always made sure our favorite foods were in the house when the grandgirls came over.

My grandma had a heart of gold and is deeply missed still to this day! We used to go shopping and always had to stop at her house to show her all the things we found good deals on. She was so excited to see what we found and always wanted us to stay for supper. It never failed she would go get her pizza delivery coupons out. Then she would tell us she was buying, and go get her "pin money" out. When we would ask her for something she would always return with, "What every your little heart desires." As I started writing this book I have heard people say this or see quotes on Pinterest saying to do "whatever your heart desires". It makes me smile when I hear or see those things, because it makes me think of what a great person my grandma was.

In the latter years she made that hard decision to move out of her house. It was a decision that took a few years, but she could not keep up with the lawn and snow removal in the winter. She moved into a senior living apartment and grumbled about the "old bitties" gossiping, but loved the music and hair dresser there. She eventually had to move into an assisted living facility and use a walker. My grandma did not want to be one of those people with a walker, she was too proud. I am not sure who talked her into it, but eventually that was how she was able to get around for a few years. Eventually she had to move into a nursing home after she fell a few times. She was in a nursing home near my parent's house when she passed away right before Christmas.

What I learned from my Grandma's funeral is that the death of a person is not just affecting you. It sounds like an obvious statement, but people are selfish when dealing with death without knowing it. (Selfish in a deserving way) I was so sad for myself and losing my grandma, until I saw my dad cry for the first time in my life at my grandma's casket. It then dawned on me that he just lost his mother! I think it was the first time that my heart was angry. It was a concept I didn't fully understand at the time.

Recently I was talking to a family friend whose mother was not doing so well. Her story reminded me a lot of my grandma's. She was telling me that her mother did not want to use a walker and did not like being in the rehabilitation facility. When she was telling me what was going on, my heart felt for her! Just knowing she was going through this and you can't fix it sucks! I gave her a big hug and just told her to enjoy her time with her now. She is still on this earth now so enjoy every moment with her mother. You cannot get time back!

Chapter 5

Children

Explaining Death to a Child

Children naturally have a million questions. When you have to explain that someone is no longer on this earth it can be tricky. It can stir up a lot of emotions when talking about the loved one who just passed away. It can be hard to come up with answers, but saying "I am not sure" is alright sometimes.

When my mother passed away our five year old had questions. She already had an understanding of death and a funeral, but about as far as a five year old can understand. I felt the need to NOT cry when she asked questions. Then she said the angel statue at our house was just like my mom, a beautiful angel! That definitely got me all teary and I thought that was amazing for her to say. That story still gets me when I think about it. Just the other day we were decorating the Christmas tree and hung an ornament on the tree that was given to us last year of an angel. Our now six year old said, "You know, I miss your mom sometimes. But she is a beautiful angel now." Again, it got me teary, and I responded, "Me too", with tears swelling in my eyes.

I remember my oldest sister talking about how she was trying not to cry when her four kids were talking about grandma passing away. Someone once told me it is alright to show emotion and cry in front of your children during a time of death. It makes them understand that it is alright for themselves to cry. It shows that their parents are human and have those feelings too. Then they too can see that their parents are going through the loss of someone as well. The concept of not crying in front of your children and being strong for them really had me thinking. I grew up with my parents never crying in front of us, except when my father cried at my grandma's funeral. That was huge; I have never seen him cry before in my entire life, made me cry even more.

Knowing that a loved one stays with you even after their soul has passed is a comforting thing. Children should know that your loved one never goes away and you can always talk to them. Explaining that they are angels in the sky is a good visual to help explain that they are with you. Keeping a photograph of the loved one and talking about fun memories they had with them is another way to help them remember. Keeping the conversion positive rather than talking about when the loved one was sick, can also help the child keep a positive memory.

Our six year old had asked if we could still have fun parties at my mom's house after she passed away. That question made me laugh! She said she always had fun there. Unfortunately we did sell the house, but fortunately we had a lot of fun there and have great memories of the time we all shared there.

Our youngest daughter always seemed to smile when she was in her bedroom, since the day she same home from the hospital. Once she started to become a little more alert she would tilt her head back and smile when we changed her diaper. Naps were never a big problem, and we could put her in her crib when she was still awake and she would fall asleep on her own. She would babble until she fell asleep and wake up babbling and in a good mood.

After going to see a medium she gave me a message from my mom, "Who do you think plays with your daughter in her room"? I think my jaw dropped! It made sense that my mom was probably there with her watching over her, talking to her, playing with her. Even thinking of it now I get tears filling my eyes. The other day I was in her room and forgot all about this picture that hangs on her wall. It was mine from when I was born. My aunt and uncle gave it to me as a birthday present. It is a picture of an angel looking over a baby lying in a crib. I remember as a young kid telling my mom that was her and the kid was me, not knowing it was a picture of an angel. Now that I look at that picture today, the angel looks a lot like my mom, and the baby looks a lot like my daughter!

The Death of a Child

Losing someone is horrific, but losing someone who was young is unfathomable to me. I personally have not lost a child or young family member like a sibling or someone close to me. I do know others who have and this is just my observation as an outsider. I do not claim to understand how they feel by any means! This is just my take on their terrible situations.

I had a friend who lost a brother in a car accident when he was about 16 years old. It was unexpected and tragic for the family. She went on to have three kids, two were boys. Her oldest son reminds me of her brother a lot with his domineer, looks and mannerisms. To some that can be a comforting thing, seeing your loved one in your child, and knowing that their spirt lives on through them. Also, her youngest son used to play in her parent's basement and would say that he would see and talk to "Little Chris". They found out the room he was playing in was Chris's old bedroom downstairs. I have heard that sometimes children can sense and "see" people who have passed.

I also had a friend who lost a child before she was full term in her pregnancy. Again, another tragic and horrific thing to go through! Nobody imagines this happy time of pregnancy can end with something so life changing and horrendous. They did name their daughter and was able to take photos to remember and honor her. A death of an infant must leave so many "whys" and questions because it is supposed to be such a joyful time. The questions and blame game starts going on for some people after the loss of a loved one.

It is only a way to beat yourself up mentally; if you can move past the questions and should haves, you can get to a point to celebrate life. Even if you only had a few short minutes or hours with a person, it was still a blessing to get pregnant, and a blessing to meet them. In order to continue with your life sanely remember to talk to your loved one because they are always there with you in spirit.

When I went to go visit the medium she said there was the spirit of a female infant near me. She went on to describe my friend's daughter. She said sometimes the sprits of children who have passed may not stick by their parents. It is only until the parent recognizes and accepts the loss that they can feel free and be by their parents. The advice she had for my friend was to talk more about her loss to friends, family members or even a counselor. She said that there are things (maybe even guilt) she could be holding onto, and that is what is hindering her from grieving. Because she is not accepting the loss her daughter is not always by her side. I did not even know what to say when she was explaining this to me. It may be true, it may not be, but that is an interesting concept that a loved one may not be by your side because you have not fully accepted the loss.

Just this past weekend I found out that my mother had a miscarriage before my oldest sister was born. I had no idea! It really had me thinking about what my parents went through at that time in their life. They were young, just married and then lost their first child. What went through their heads? How did they feel? How did they move on? So many questions I have that I will never have the opportunity to ask them now. Then my questions shifted to, why didn't they every tell me? If that child was born, would I have never been born? I am the youngest of four girls and the closest age is ten years ranging up to 15 years between my oldest sister. It is safe to assume I was an oops I think. How would holiday's be different? Why did this happen to my parents? Would we have had an older brother or sister? A lot of unanswered questions that I do not really have answers to.

Chapter 6

A Friend...gone

A Friend

This morning I saw on Facebook a college friend of mine passed away unexpectedly. It does not say how, when or any details, just that it is confirmed he has passed away. It is super shocking and doesn't seem real to me. I have not spoken to him in a few years and was not extremely close to him, but he was part of our group of friends. He always had a smile on his face, and always had something nice and funny to say. He was a super smart guy who graduated in the Art program at college, and all around great person. So it is just so surreal that he is now gone from this earth, and it just doesn't seem fair.

He would be about 30 years old and that seems way too early to be taken from this earth. Death just seems so final. I know that is an obvious statement, but it is just such an eerie feeling that a person is just gone. I am not sure if today is just a reminder for me about death, but I just feel so terrible for the family and what they have to go through in the next few days.

I was thinking about my parents last night and how I wish they would have met certain people. I wish they were around so I could call them just to talk, just to get an opinion on something, to hear their laugh, so many things. At the bottom of the Facebook post my friend's cousin posted, she mentioned to hug your loved ones. That is one thing that is very true; tell your friends and family how much you love them, because you never know. Death can pop up to anyone at any time. It is so final it is creepy and absolutely heartbreaking and sad!

I was just thinking back on memories of him in college and they were always of him smiling and laughing. He was such a happy-go-lucky guy. A few of us went swimming on a summer day and we get in the lake about waste deep and you hear him say, "Awe man". We looked over and he pulled his wallet and Cellphone out of his swimsuit pockets, soaking wet! He just started laughing, wasn't made like most people. He just said, "I can't believe I did that", and continued to laugh. It just seems so unfair sometimes that the best people are taken from this world and leaving a lot of people hurt and with no explanation of why this had to happen.

I think that a lot of grieving people struggle with the "why". That was a big one for me and still is. Why do both of my parents have to be gone? Why did my dad have to die when I was 23? Why did my mom have to die when she was so healthy? Why do I not have parents anymore, but other people who do not appreciate theirs still have parents? Why did this super happy friend have to be taken from this earth when he provided so much joy to others?

A Cousin

I have a friend Debbie who suffered a few big losses in her life in a short period of time. Around that time Debbie had also lost a cousin due to suicide. Her family always was a close knit family and she was pretty close with her cousin. Her family is making a documentary about her cousin's life to raise awareness for suicide prevention. I think it is an amazing thing for her family to do! I had asked her if she would like to share what the hardest part of that loss was, and here was her answer:

> "With so much publicity, at one point I felt like I no longer was remembering "my cousin". I had all this outside information and views into his life that I didn't have while he was alive that "my cousin" felt lost. Suicide is such a taboo topic that it's hard to explain why his situation had been so "important" or influential. People have very set opinions on suicide that sometimes I feel hesitant to express my grief. Example: I want people to watch his documentary because he meant so much TO ME, his story personally affected me...but it's hard to approach that subject with anyone who did not grow up with me, and knew him because it's immediately about the suicide/anxiety/depression topic (which is also important but is usually a secondary reasoning for me)". Debbie said.

My condolences still go out to her family; he was such a great kid and you could tell he loved his family very much. I do think it is a very important topic and hopefully his story will help many kids going through the same thing! I didn't realize that the raising awareness of his death could hinder or affect someone's grieving process because it is so publicized and talked about. It does make sense though, almost like the compassion for that individual is diluted and the topic is about suicide and not the loss of that person.

Chapter 7

Death of a Pet

Debbie also had her only dog pass away as well. Pets can be members of a family just like a human to a lot of people. Wherever Debbie went the dog went too. He was such a great dog, probably close to 80 pounds but he thought he was a lap dog. He loved to play and run outside, but if anyone was on the couch he would cuddle up with you. Basically one of those great dogs you do not see that often, one that you wish you had. Unfortunately Debbie witnessed her dog running across the street and getting unexpectedly hit by a car. She was the only one home and had to deal with the tragic situation. I still do not know how she did it that day, she was and is a very strong person for going through that!

I asked her what the hardest part was after she lost her dog, this was her response: "Realizing what a major part of my life/time was spent with and/or planning for him. Changing my routine as I no longer needed extra time that was dedicated to his care. Also feeling slightly embarrassed about how deeply affected I was by "just a pet"." She said. Losing a person or a pet leaves gaps in your life or extra time where you did things for that person in your daily routine. I remember her saying she didn't know what to do with herself that she didn't have to load up her dog in the morning before work or go pick him up after work. She didn't have to go take him for a walk every day. When she left for a weekend she didn't have to figure out where he was going to stay if she couldn't bring him along. That sense of emptiness but gained free time was bittersweet.

Recently I just found out another friend Drechel lost a pet too. She did not tell anyone because it was too painful to talk about without tearing up. Pets are like children for some people. They go and do everything with their owners. So when a pet passes away it is like a death of a human to them. When I read that Drechel's dog passed away I started to tear up! He was a great dog, just a little fluff ball that thought he was tough. You could take him on a walk and he would walk all proud with his head held high. Then he would go pee on every tree you passed. I doggy sat him a couple times when I quit my job, and I would go let him out during the day and play with him. Such a good dog with a little under bite, he will be missed! Drechel mentioned that losing a pet isn't the same as a child, but if you do not have children they sure do mean the world to you.

Chapter 8

Selling our Childhood Home

People can grieve over the loss of a relationship, the loss of a job, a family home, a pet, so many different things. When your life was "normal" and something was taken from it there is that hole you may not know how to fill. Just remember that others in similar situations (nobody will have gone through the same thing as you), were able to still live normal lives and learn how to cope and get through it.

After my parents both passed away all three of my sisters and I had to clean out my parent's house and put it on the market to be sold. First off dealing with the death of your last parent is emotional and devastating enough, then add going through all of your childhood memories and saying goodbye to where you grew up- now that is tough! There were a lot of laughs and a lot of tears, both good and bad.

I still get emotional thinking about that house being cut out of our lives. I tend to see that house and the rooms in it, in some of my dreams so I have found comfort in that. It is still sad it is not "mom and dad's house" anymore. No more cookouts there, no more Thanksgivings or Christmas', my youngest daughter never had a holiday there. I find myself driving past there every now and then just to see it again. It usually brings back some memories, more painful at first, but it has gotten better now. Now when I drive past I almost smile thinking about the fun memories instead of the loss of the house.

That house was bought by my parent's right after they were married and all three of my sisters and I grew up there. Our parents had the house for 46 years. My dad added a porch, kitchen and two bedrooms upstairs. We all helped build the 2 tier deck in the back yard and each had a turn painting the inside of the shed or "club house" whatever color we wanted. I bounced a lot of tennis balls off the garage roof trying to catch them. I colored the crap out of that driveway in the summers with chalk. When my nephews were little they covered every inch also. My dad taught each of us how to change a tire on a vehicle in that driveway. Come to find out we think he just wanted his snow tires on the truck so it was his "lesson" for us. We had to practice a total of 4 times until all the tires were changed. Weird how it didn't dawn on us that was his plan all along until.... 20 years later. Well played dad, well played!

Grieving the loss of a house is not something people tend to talk about or discuss. Even doing a search online there is not much information out there of people talking about it. Maybe it is something that is not that common, or just not talked about because it is something tangible or material thing that was lost. That house was our home and it was the memories or the place we created memories in for many years. I think that was the hardest part, there was not going to be that common meeting ground anymore. Also, with that came the loss of my mother at the same time so it was a double whammy.

I had a friend whose parents sold their childhood home and built a home near it. I asked her if it was sad seeing her childhood home when she went to visit her parents. I remember her telling me that it was a little sad. She said she could see it, but you can't go into it. There were so many memories and get togethers there, but you can't go back into it.

With every other type of loss time seems to help, that hurt and sadness has turned into smiles and memories. I am glad we have photos of all of my siblings in the house when we were young (even the embarrassing ones). It helps on those days when sadness may come back to laugh and the good times and the ridiculous plaid couches!

Chapter 9

Struggling

**"She was drowning,
but nobody saw her struggle."
-Unknown**

If life seems unmanageable, you are sick of feeling terrible all the time or you question your worth on this earth, you probably need help from someone other than yourself. I am not a psychologist or doctor, but I have lived all of those thoughts and feelings after my dad passed away. My life got to the point where my boyfriend at the time broke up with me in a note because he didn't know how to help me anymore. The note said I should seek professional help. That was an awakening for me. I thought I was managing my life just fine. I thought I did not need to pay someone to talk to me, who does not know me. How was that supposed to make me feel better or even help?

The more I thought about it I realized what I had been doing to get by apparently was not working. I was to the point where I internalized everything. I did not really talk about my dad passing away to people. I did not talk to my family as much because it brought back memories. When I did talk to them they were sad conversations, and who wanted to deal with that? I was not showering every day because that seemed like a lot of work. I would go out to the bars a few nights a week because that was fun and who wanted to be sad? I would cry at night or just lay in bed when I got home from work and watch TV or a movie and just cry. Previous to my dad passing away I was not a crier at all, so this was new to me.

There were two distinct points I remember having an odd experience. I now know they were anxiety attacks. The first one happened when I was in a college class and I opened a bottle of soda and it fizzed all over my desk and made a big noise. Everyone from the class stopped and looked at me. We were seated in a horeshoe shape so all eyes were pointed at me and it was really quiet. For some reason my face turned bright read, it felt so hot. I remember almost like it wasn't me. I looked at the door and wanted to escape, but couldn't move. It almost felt like I was trapped and was freaking out. That moment was similar to the second anxiety attack. I remember walking down the stairs of my work and my legs started getting wobbly and my vision started narrowing down almost like there was black in my peripheral vision every time I blinked. The hallway started to get smaller and smaller and my breathing increased. I booked it to the bathroom and just sat in a stall trying to breath for a long time. Those were moments that were in the beginning of my struggle and things progressed a little worse.

At one point I was living in an apartment by myself, quit my job and was starting to get behind on my bills. I have never actually told anyone about this, but at a few points my electricity was shut off. One point just before it started to get cold in the winter when the electricity was disconnected; my water was also shut off. I remember flushing the toilet with flat 2 liter bottles of soda. I remembering thinking that something had to change if I could not find a job, too broke to turn my electricity and water back on. Somewhere deep down I knew my life was not supposed to be like this. I wanted a richer existence, I wanted to live a life that was not sad, that could get through life like everyone else. My pride was too big to ask for help though. So I sold my dad's truck, paid off my bills and decided to move back to my hometown- which ended up being the best decision of my life.

I really do not know if it was that break up note or what it was that gave me that push contact a counselor, but I am very glad I did. I knew I needed to change my thoughts from negative to positive, and nobody else was going to do it for me. After my first session at a behavioral health center in the town I was living, it gave me a new outlook on how I was feeling. I had read blogs and books and tried to relate my story with other people's stories and I just couldn't. Nobody had that special relationship with MY dad and nobody was in the same situation I was when he died. Talking to a professional showed me that I had situational Depression and that is a common thing. Suddenly I didn't feel as alone and started to realize the things I did have going for me. It made me find out all my internal thoughts building up was causing me to develop situational Depression and Anxiety Disorder. **"You've seen my decent. Now watch me rising." -Rumi**

Throughout a few months to a year I tried multiple different prescriptions to help me get on the right track and deal with my grief in a healthier way. I am not saying prescriptions are the way to go, but just talking to a professional even on the phone may help you a 100 times more than doing what you were doing. This is the way I look at it now- what is the worst that can happen if you call a professional they will tell you that your thoughts and feelings are normal, or they will say you shouldn't be feeling like this and we can talk about a plan together to get you on the right track. If you are embarrassed about asking for help, nobody has to know. You can call a counselor and they will not know who you are and if you want you do not have to talk to them again. I believe that going to talk to someone really did help me in many ways. It got me out of the funk and helped point me in the right direction of my now amazing life.

I always wanted to know how long am I going to have this feeling of sadness and when will it go away. Brace yourself if you have not heard this statistic yet, the average time to grieve a loss is five years. Eek! Yup, that sounds so long and who wants to feel that deep down sadness and reminders for five years?! Let me tell you it is different for everyone and in every situation. Looking back it did take almost five years for me to fully grieve the loss of my father. That does not mean that I don't miss him or think of him every day, but it does mean that I learned to replace that horrific hurt with happy memories and feelings.

Grieving the loss of my mother took close to a year, but a lot was crammed into that year and going through the death of a parent once before helped me understand this grief a little more. I did have to grieve the loss of having no parents and our childhood home at the same time as well, all while being pregnant with my first child. I used to get mad at the "10 Step Process of Grieving", I would skip over that section in grieving books or when reading other people's blogs. Maybe it was my stubbornness, independent self that thought nobody can tell me how I am going to go through this process, maybe I skipped some steps, and maybe I won't go through all of those steps. Looking back I did go through those steps, with my father a lot slower than with my mother's death, but I did go through them.

I really liked this quote I came across out of the blue, "**I wasn't prepared for the fact that grief is so unpredictable. It wasn't just sadness, and it wasn't linear**". **– Meghan O'Rourke** It makes complete sense to me, the first time I went through a big loss I just wanted to know when that feeling would be over. It was a little bit, then something triggered a sad or outburst of crying moment and I was back to grieving. Life and sadness absolutely does get better with time and so does your mental health, but it can be a rollercoaster. Cling to those around you or cling to those similar stories online that provide you that hope that others got through it.

I remember that year after my dad passed away my mom mailed me a book and it was extremely helpful, it wasn't about grief it was about grace. It was the book *The Unmistakable Touch of Grace*, by Cheryl Richardson. There was something about that book that I was really drawn to. Maybe because it was part of the steps I took to get me out of the funk I was in. Or it could have been because I kept seeing the words Grace appear everywhere all of a sudden. She had suffered a loss of a relationship and wrote about what she did to move on from there. Something about that book spoke to me and I reread it a few times since that day. I appreciate my mom for sending that book to me out of the blue and still have that same copy today on my bookshelf. Another resource she mentioned in her book was the Touch of Grace cards at www.cherylrichardson.com I would check back on this website every now and then to see if there was some new inspiring message just for me. I just clicked on it as I write this and woo that was spot on for me! I encourage anyone to check it out if that interests you.

"Most humans are never fully present in the now, because unconsciously they believe that the next moment must be more important than this one. But then you miss your whole life, which is never not now. And that's a revelation for some people: to realize that your life is only ever now." –Eckhart Tolle. Take charge of your life today and realize that looking back or forward in life is not fully living. If you are struggling with what happened in your past or how you will get through your future, you need to appreciate that you are living your life right now. What you chose to do with your life right now matters more than what was or what will be. Reading this book is one step in living your life for right now. Seeking professional help such as a support group or counseling is living in the now to better your future. If that quote really resonates with you I suggest checking out some of Eckahart Tolle's quotes online or any of his books, they were very thought-provoking to me. If you cannot tell by now I am a huge quote person. **"When something bad happens you have three choices. You can either let it define you. Let it destroy you, or you can let it strengthen you." -Unknown** Looking back I know I was broken.

"Where there is deep grief, there was deep love." –Zig Ziglar Whether it is someone else struggling or even you, I hope you can find some comfort in knowing that deep grief and struggle is a result of a deep love. Love is a beautiful thing and the highest frequency we can be at, not everyone finds that type of love in their lives, so you were one of the lucky ones to have experienced that relationship with that person. Yes, they are no longer here physically, but the time you had with them was beautiful and something not everyone can say they had.

Chapter 10

Guilt

Not Able To Say Goodbye

I have also grieved the concept of not being able to say goodbye to my parents, mainly my dad. When my dad passed away I lived on the other side of the state about four hours away and did not have a car at the time. After getting that mind-blowing, unreal, life altering phone call I was mad at the fact that my sisters and my mom could all be right there and say good bye, but I could not. I did not get to see my father until the day of the funeral. That was still the hardest thing I have ever done in my entire life- walk from the back of the church up to the casket. I tend to replay that memory a lot when I start to get apprehensive about doing something that I am a little scared of, I tell myself "If I made that walk up to the casket, I can do anything else". I remember having a breakdown and sobbing on my sisters shoulder.

Recently I went to see a Medium/Psychic to see what it was all about and in hopes that my parents would come through to talk to

Gina Schampers

me. Either you believe in mediums, are skeptical, or think they are a hoax, to each their own. I say if you can get anything out of a message go with it, and I did. She had told me that my dad said to talk to him more, and tell him all the things I never was able to say. That is one thing I still have not done, I am not sure why. Maybe I think it will hurt too much and all of those feelings will come rushing back? I am working on it though. Baby steps tend to help ease me into it.

The medium also asked me if I was unable to say goodbye, which was true!. He said for my own sanity I need to talk to him and tell him what eats at me, and tell him the things I was not able to say the day he died. I did not realize I was still holding on to that after six years. The more I thought about it though it still gets to me that I wasn't back home and able to say goodbye. I felt guilty, mad and a lot of other emotions about that day. In a way I almost felt cheated out of that closure that my sisters and mom might have had that day, which I was never able to experience.

Knowing someone else is going through grieving after you have suffered a loss is more heart aching than before going through it yourself. To me it is ten times worse now when I see a friend or loved one go through a loss, just knowing how much it really does hurt and affect your life. It is something that you would not wish upon your worst enemy, but I think it helps to be more compassionate, understanding and helpful for that loved one during the difficult time. Often people are unsure of what to say or do and feel uncomfortable when someone loses a person. If you have gone through it yourself you might have that urge to reach out quicker or really want to send flowers or a meal.

After my father passed away I had friends who have also unfortunately lost parents. I have told them anytime they just need to talk or bounce ideas off of me do it. Sometimes you feel that others do not understand because they have not suffered a loss as significant or similar to yours. I have felt compelled to send grief books to friends in hopes that they would bring some sort of comfort or understanding for them. (Yup, I'm talking about you Jolene). Even asking how a person is doing a week or a month after the passing is very important. A lot of friends and loved ones forget that you are not back to a "normal" life and it still affects you every day, even if you do not talk about it. That follow up to make sure a person is alright is HUGE. After the funeral or burial the overflow of support tends to dissipate and may make a person feel that people do not care, which it is not the case, but it can feel that way to a person who has suffered a loss.

Losing someone really makes a person think, if you were not in your head before a loss you most likely will be after a loss. The "life is short" comment really resonates with you. You start thinking about your own life expectancy. Maybe even question why you are here and what your purpose on this life is. Why are people taken away so quickly when they had so many plans and things they wanted to do? After losing both my parents it is really starting to hit home with me that I need to be doing something for other people or helping others. I am not sure why, maybe it was the nature of my mother and all the volunteering she did, or the realization that we have some purpose on this life and I am not sure what that is exactly. I was listening to an audiobook in my car the other day about a book called *Happier,* by Tal Ben Shahar and he said something along the lines of, **"Life is too short for the "have-to's" to hardly make time for the "want-to's""** I started to think about my current job and what I want to spend my time and energy on going forward.

Accepting a Loss

Sometimes I also wonder why am I OK with and have accepted that both of my parents are gone. It is almost a guilty feeling, that I should be crying or grieving more, but I have reached the point of "it is what it is" and life continues without that person there no matter what. Lately I have been reflecting on why I feel so guilty about being alright. You would think that it is a relief to not have that anger or crying stage going on. I am at peace with the thoughts that they are still with me no matter what and that they are safe and ok. The only thing I can think of is that maybe I see that my sisters have not fully grieved yet and they are not ok with the situation yet, but I am. I know I have to release that guilty feeling to fully move on as well, but it is hard sometimes.

Damn those compassionate feelings! I know they will get to my point at some time in their life, but why did I get there so quickly? The death of a person, pet or relationship sometimes never stops with the questions, but you just have to learn how to keep moving forward in life. "**Grief changes us, the pain sculpts us into someone who understands more deeply, hurts more often, appreciates more quickly, cries more easily, hopes more desperately, loves more openly.**" –**Unknown.** Sometimes going through a devastating loss can make you a stronger more compassionate person. Yes, it could have been extremely painful to take, but you made it through and have a deeper understanding of life and feelings because of it. Death can help us grow as a person mentally and emotionally, maybe take some turns up and down about a million times, but reflecting on what you have learned is an important part of the process. Death and loss sucks, it sucks a lot, but how you go through it can easy or hard depending on how you deal with it. Like I mentioned in the beginning there is no right or wrong way to grieve and nobody can tell you how. This is just my story and how I view the process after suffering some major losses in my life.

There is a period after a person passes away, at least for me, that you feel numb. Basically it is like you're just going through the motions of the days to get through. There is sadness there for the loss, but it does not really set it in right away the reality of that loss and hole in your life now. Eventually the reality of the situation hit me and then a lot of emotions came rushing at once. With my dad I buried those feelings and pushed them away, with my mom I was more open to talking about it and worked through it will the selling of the house.

Chapter 11

Growing Up From Death

Became an Adult

I just recently heard someone ask, "When did you realize you were an adult?" Most of the time I feel like I am still a kid or a kid pretending to be an adult, so it took me awhile to reflect and find the answer. It then dawned on me that I truly became an adult when both of my parents had passed away. There was nobody like your parents to call when you have a question, nobody like your parents to be your backup in case something goes wrong, nobody like your parents to give you advice or even a hug and tell you it will be alright. Your older generation is deceased, and you are the next in line- that is a scary realization!

I have learned from my mother's sudden passing that a person can be taken away from you in a second without any warning. You always hear those stories, but never ever think it would happen to you. When it does it is shocking, life altering and unbelievable. So many emotions, thoughts and feelings come rushing to you in waves.

That holy crap moment when you remember you do not have parents anymore can be a huge issue by itself. Unfair thoughts can take over; the need to better yourself because you do not have that backup or parents to rely on, more unfair thoughts, scared feelings, a sense of being lost so many things can come rushing to you.

Adult Orphan

The term orphaned adult seems very fitting to me to describe how I feel about both parents passing. I don't say that to get pitty by any means, but because it is the best way to describe how I feel. Both of my parents and all grandparents no longer on this earth and there is not anyone directly older than me. Nobody "owns" you anymore, you do not have that bloodline to fall back on for help, you are on your own and are physically without parents. That is a scary concept to grasp. If you fall into this category my suggestion to you is to talk to other siblings, significant other, coworker, anyone you can confide in to talk it out. This is still a concept I cannot get out of my mind and a tricky one for me to shake. I do not know if it is the age or the shock of it all, I still have not figured it out yet, but I do at times feel like an adult orphan.

Life/Career Change as a Result

I have got to the point in my current career/job where it almost feels pointless with the work that I am doing. Meetings about projects and the unnecessary stress at work just does not seem worth my sanity anymore. It is a tricky situation for me to be in because ever since I was in Middle School I have had this drive to work towards a degree and job in sports marketing. That was my goal and nothing was going to stop me. Well, as of recently that does not seem like the career I am supposed to be doing or I am not able to help enough people doing that job. It is a real struggle for me to accept that because once I get on a path and tell everyone to just wait I am going to do it- then just stop that dream I have had for 15 years, I feel like I am failing or giving up.

My new outlook on my current situation is to just to let it go, as hard as that is. If a better opportunity is supposed to come along it will present itself in my path. I am not saying to everyone going through a loss quit your job and do something else. I just wanted to point out that in my current situation it made me re-evaluate what I was doing on a daily basis and pivot to hopefully do something that can reach and help people on a large scale.

Chapter 12

Love

Two things I realize happen when a person passes away. 1. You see the unbelievable love and support of your friends and family during a difficult time. 2. You see the love and lives an individual touched throughout their lifetime. Both are amazing, heartwarming and touching!

Support

> **"Family isn't always blood. It's the people in your life who want you in theirs; the ones who accept you for who you are. The ones who would do anything to see your smile and who love you no matter what."**
>
> **–Unknown**

So many cards and messages saying, "let me know if there is anything I/we can do for you", people who brought over food, people who brought food to the lunch after mass at the church, flowers that were sent, hugs from people, cards, so much support shows up with you don't expect it. It was touching both times with my mother and father's deaths to see family and friends reach out and show their support. Sometimes I did not know how to respond to those messages or offers from people. I have found that if you do not respond people understand completely, you have a lot going on! In a way I think people just reaching out makes them feel like they are helping in some way.

During the passing of my mother, my boyfriend was there every step of the way without even asking him. I think that is a hard spot to be in, being that support for a significant other and seeing how much they are hurting. The best advice I can give (everyone is different, but this is what helped me) is just to be there. He did not have to say anything just having him there at the hospital for that week, putting his hand on my back when we were in the waiting room, being there for me to cry on his shoulder at night, he never had to say anything ever. Him being there for me was more than enough.

I cannot thank him enough for what he did that week and every day since then. That is a tough spot to be in and you never know if you should be there, or the person wants you there. My advice is just go and be there, if the person does not want you there they will tell you. For the record I did want him there for many reasons, he is probably reading this thinking, "Crap, did I do the right thing?" Yes he did more than the right thing and I cannot thank him enough for being there for me and having to go through that with my sisters and I, same with my brother-in law.

They had to put up with the four sisters crying hysterically one minute, to laughing until we had tears the next minute, to goofing around because we were all so exhausted. They both should get an award for sitting in a hospital waiting room for a week, if you would have seen us by that last day you probably thought we belonged on the Psych floor. I think at one point my sister found the big floor cleaning machine and pretended to use it until we noticed what she was doing- yup we got to that level of weirdness by the end. At the same time it was therapy for us to laugh in a time of sorrow. **"A family that grieves together heals together." -Unknown**

Lives They Touched

The people and messages that came and still come from the lives both of my parents have touched are amazing. Thinking about it makes me get a little teary- in a good way. My father was a teacher and a very chatty man, he would leave to go to the grocery store for milk and come back two hours later. No joke, this happened probably once a week if not more. He would get to talking to someone he knew and lose track of time. He knew everyone, so it was no surprise when the whole world showed up at his funeral. What my family did not see coming was the amount of people who showed up for my mother's funeral. She was an AMAZING lady, did everything she could for her family, felt guilty buying a pair of shoes for herself when she should have spent that money on something or someone else. She volunteered for everything under the sun and had a goofy personality that made you just love her.

When she passed unexpectedly we thought that there would be less people than my dad's funeral (because my dad knew everyone), so that is what we went off of when we ordered food for the lunch after the mass. Well what we learned was that my mom also knew EVERYONE under the sun and more. More people showed up for my mother's funeral than my father's! We heard stories from people she delivered Meals on Wheels to, from the "Quilting Ladies", from the "Community 2000 Ladies", from people she volunteered with at St. Vincent DePaul, from members of the church that she was involved in, from childhood friends, so many people we had no idea who some people were.

We knew she was a busy lady because you could never get ahold of her, but it was so heartwarming to hear all of the people she had touched mainly from volunteering. She loved helping people and my sisters and I decided to donate all of the money from her funeral to all of her favorite charities and places she used to volunteer at. It is exactly what she would have done!

The love and support of her friends and the community went beyond just the day of the funeral. After my daughter was born the Community 2000 ladies had a gift for our daughter. They all signed a card and wrote congratulations "From Grandma's friends at 2000" along with a really nice fleece blanket they made. To this day that blanket is still the one we use in her crib tucked in like a sheet. She loves it. I thought that was such a sweet thing they did after the funeral was over, they had never met me besides at the funeral, but they knew how excited my mom was for another grandbaby.

Chapter 13

What to Say or Do

When you see someone else struggling it is human nature to try to help, especially when it is close friends of family members. I lived across the state when my father died so I was not near to see it first-hand how my mother was doing. I know when I came back from college on weekends she had been busy painting the house, organizing things, cleaning, doing house projects and all kinds of things. Might have been therapeutic for her or maybe it was a way to just keep busy so she wasn't alone in a quiet house where she used to share it with my dad, I am not sure. I remember my mom talking about how she finally went to go talk to a councilor that someone in the church referred her to. My sisters were around to make sure she was doing alright and keep checking on her and doing this with her, wouldn't let her go up north to our cabin alone for a long time, so I assumed she was doing alright. I will never know now if she really was doing alright inside, but we turned part of our energy on making sure she was doing alright.

Gina Schampers

I found out that one of her close friends used to mail her a card around the anniversary of my dad's passing. That to me brought tears to my eyes. Getting something like that is worth a million hugs to me. It shows that a person still thinks about you and what you are going through. After the first few months the condolences seem to disappear and everyone goes back to their normal lives, but you don't. After one of my friends father's passed away I made it a point to text her every day just to check in. I knew if she didn't want to respond she wouldn't. A few years later she thanked me saying that those texts really helped her get through that rough time. Sending that simple, "thinking about you", or "how are you today" can mean the world to someone going through a loss.

I attended the funerals of two of my close friend's parents. I remember not knowing what to say at the first funeral. I did not go through something like she just did. I felt terrible for her, my heart ached and I wanted to make it better. I didn't know what to say, but most people don't and that is ok. Showing up for support means a lot! At my mom's funeral one of my college friends I saw standing in line who I did not see for a few years. Right then and there I started crying. It was so touching that even after a few years he took time out of his day to travel there just to give me a hug. That meant so much to me!

After one of my close friends father passed away I made it a point to text her every day for a few months. I'm not saying do this because the next person who has a family member pass away will get 50 texts a day, but in this situation it was apparently what she needed. At that time my father had passed away too so I could talk from my experience. I remember her speaking at her father's funeral and thinking, how can you do that? She seemed so calm and it was such a brave thing for her to do. She had me in tears in the audience. It was seeing that, that gave me the courage to speak at my mother's funeral. It is something I am very glad I did and I only did it because I saw how courageous she was, and I thank you for that Leslie!

Nothing a person can say or do will lessen the pain, I wish at times I could take away the pain a person goes through when dealing with a death because it is not fun. It sucks, it's sad, you are left with a hole in your heart and life, and nothing can ever fill that void except memories. But what you can do for a person going through a loss is to be there for them, tell them you love them, embrace them, tell them you are there to listen or lend an ear. Hearing "I understand what you are going through," is probably the worst thing to say. Even if you have lost the same parent or both parents it is not the same, which is a good way to have a person shy away from you. In the moment you think that nobody can understand what you're going through, nobody can understand your relationship YOU had with that person. It will never be the same; you don't have that person to call up when you have a question, or that person to share your funny inside jokes with anymore.

Chapter 14

Triggers and Holidays

"There are moments in life when you miss
someone so much that you just want to pick
them from your dreams and hug them for real."
–Charlie Brown

Triggers

Songs are giant triggers for me when it comes to the death of loved ones. For about a year I could not listen to a Johnny Cash song without tearing up, having to leave the room, or change the song without thinking of my dad. On about year two it was iffy if I would cry or not, now I get happy and the songs remind me of my dad. When I hear Charlie Pride especially "Kiss An Angel Good Morning", it still gets me a little bit and I think about my mom. Charlie Pride was her absolute favorite singer and she would always sing out loud when his songs came on. When I hear his songs I also hear my mom singing along too, it is a bittersweet feeling.

Sometimes songs I have even forgotten about will come on and I will freeze for a second because my memory shoots right over to that loved one that passed away. That happened to me a few weeks ago with some country song I cannot even remember the name of came on the radio and I froze for a second. I love holiday music but there is one particular song that is one I cannot listen to anymore. My Grandma passed away in a nursing home right before Christmas and the workers said when she passed away Silent Night was playing. That was about 6 years ago, going on 7 and I still have to walk out of a room or turn the station when that song comes on. I used to love that song but I always get a mental picture of her passing away closing her eyes. It is a peaceful thought, but it will make me cry no matter what if I hear the whole song.

I have had my fair share of breakdowns at some inappropriate moments in my life. If that has ever happened to you do not worry, nobody is going to remember that you had a breakdown five years from now. Just know that it is your body and mind's way of releasing your emotions. It is just too bad my breakdowns didn't have better timing, but oh well it is in the past.

Many times at work or in a meeting I have had an unexpected breakdown. The biggest breakdowns came at the year anniversary mark of the death of my parents. The one year marker for my dad I had to take off of work, it was just bad. Mentally I was not in a good place and basically cried and could not function that day. When year two came around I took off of work to just be safe and I was fine, year three I did not take off of work and I had a breakdown at work that day. With my mother the one year anniversary really was not that bad, I got teary at work, but did not have a meltdown. Others I know who have suffered a significant loss (not just a death) have had a hard time with the one year anniversary mark. It seems normal to feel that way, your human and it is only natural to reflect on what your life was like a year ago and think about the events that took place that terrible, terrible day.

Holidays

Holidays are another iffy one. After the death of a loved one, a loss of something, or a pet, holidays just are not the same. That one person may have had a tradition that just does not feel right to do without them there. Or they might have always gave a funny gift, or gave goofy hints as to what was wrapped up, now there is that huge hole in the holidays and it just does not feel "normal" anymore. I love holidays because we get to spend them with family and it is always a fun and enjoying time. It is definitely not the same compared to when I was younger or even a few years ago, but it is my "new normal" for holidays. Things change every year as my sisters and I are adjusting to holidays without parents and trying to start new traditions. Starting new traditions seems to be what we are doing lately, but for our kids and my nephews and niece it is starting to be their new normal too.

My dad would always get excited about holidays. For Halloween he would count how many trick or treaters came to the door each year and write it down on a cupboard board in his garage. He loved to see how many we had from year to year and which ones were "big candy years". He wrote everything down on the walls and cupboard doors of that garage. We always joked that if that garage ever burned down my dad would be lost. He had what was planted in the garden, how many plants grew and where in the garden written down. When we were packing everything up from the house my oldest sister took the cupboard door off and kept it. It was our family's way of keeping a piece of my dad and a piece of his garage. We still joke about the crazy things he kept track of in that garage. The new owners probably thought some goofy kid was let lose in there and just started writing on the walls.

My dad loved to give gifts, mainly at Christmas time. I know who I take after with gift giving, I would rather give a gift than get one any day. I just get so excited and love to give hints and give presents early. It turns out my dad was the same way, but just a little bit goofier. I remember every year we would get hints about our Christmas presents like, "Looks like everything comes in yellow this year", "You could probably use your Christmas present right about now", "I hope you like polka dots", "Your feet look cold, you probably wish you had your Christmas present". I find myself doing the same thing now and giving little hints.

I was shopping with one of my sisters recently and we were talking about gift giving. This year I have almost all of my Christmas shopping done by October. Every time I see those bags hidden I really want to give something to someone. I have been a little guilty of doing that already this year...woops. My sister told me that when they were really little apparently my dad would let them play with their Christmas gifts a month ahead of time then pack them away and wrap them up for Christmas. I guess he couldn't wait either!

For Christmas and Easter it was the two times of the year that our entire family went to church, including my dad. For Christmas I always remember him bringing hard candy along because it sounded so loud when he unwrapped it in the quiet church. If it was not too cold we would walk up to church, but if it was cold we would drive. The Christmas masses we drove my dad always had to bring us around the neighborhood to look at the Christmas lights. He always got excited when there was an impressive looking house. To this day I still LOVE to look at Christmas lights anywhere I am. There is something about it that makes me smile. I'm a sucker for a nicely lit house. The last few years around Christmas time I have taken the oldest one around to look at lights in the neighborhood when it gets dark.

Chapter 15

The Lighter Side-
Meatballs and Memories

Memories are what slowly fill the holes in a broken heart after a loss or death. Remembering the joy that person brought to you and those happy times you shared can turn the hurt into smiles. **"Sometimes you will never know the value of a moment until it becomes a memory." –Dr. Suess.** Thinking back on some great memories of my parents and grandparents these are some of my favorite memories.

Grandma and the Meatballs

My Grandma did a lot of funny things, but one story stands out that still makes me giggle to myself even now writing it. One winter she had a pan of meatballs that she did not want to throw in the garbage for some reason so she decided to dispose of them in another way. It was wintertime and it had just snowed so she thought it was a good idea to go throw the meatballs in a bush. Well after the snow melted the neighbors saw a bunch of meatballs in their bush and got mad. Turns out when my grandma threw the meatballs in the bush (still have no idea why she thought this was a good idea) they flew into the next bush that belonged to the neighbors. The next day she was talking to the neighbors and they were complaining about some punk kids in the neighborhood who threw meatballs in their bush and now it stinks!

My grandma was so embarrassed she didn't want to say anything and years later told us this story. She was saying she hopes nobody saw her throw the meatballs in the bush or they might think she is an "Arse Hole!". Can you imagine seeing a little old lady carrying a frying pan of meatballs and chucking them into a snowy bush then walking back into her house like that is normal?! Oh it makes me laugh every time!

My Mom and the Meatballs

My mom had an incident with meatballs as well that we never let her live down when she was alive. She is probably shaking her head at me from heaven right now for telling this story- Sorry Mom, but it is too funny not to share! Our family liked to playfully tease each other all the time. One day my mom was throwing out leftovers from the fridge which she rarely ever did, if there was leftovers they were meant to be eaten. She did not want to throw them in the garbage either so her solution was to flush them down the toilet. Well, that did not work out in her favor. Turns out it clogged the toilet pretty bad and she could not get it unstuck with the plunger. She was plunging like crazy getting red in the face, mainly mad at what she did, but also because the damn things were stuck and wouldn't come out.

My dad came in the house giggling to himself with this big long rod in his hand. Picture Santa Clause with the white beard and belly who was usually very somber and stoic giggling with the thing he called a "turd buster" in his hands. He came in and said, "Watch out I've got the turd buster to get your meatballs out!" still giggling to himself. All four of us girls were laughing our heads off at this situation and the fact that our dad called it the turd buster. Anytime she cooked meatballs after that we joked around that she better not flush them down the toilet or dad would have to get out the turd buster. She hated it, but I think it did make her laugh a little. So now when I cook meatballs I think of those 2 stories every time!

Memories

A voice is a big memory of a person that I hope I never lose the memory of a loved one who has passed away. I have heard other people say they cannot remember a person's voice after they have passed away and that makes them feel disconnected. Photos can be a great memory trigger if you cannot remember a person's voice. My mom's voice stands out the most to me because when I hear certain songs on the radio I distinctly hear her singing along with them. Her voice always stood out when she would sing along to the radio. I am not sure why maybe because it was a little off from the singers, or she would sing louder than the radio, or that there was so much joy in her voice when she sang along to those songs on the radio. Whatever it was it is a great memory I have of my mother. When those certain songs come on like, "Kiss an Angel Good Morning," by Charlie Pride, "The Dance" by Garth Brooks, "Please Send Some Snow for Johnny," or certain Christmas songs I can hear my mom plain as day signing right along to those songs.

A voice can come through from someone else. Last year we were setting up the baptism of our youngest daughter and I was coordinating everything with the church. I had a phone call from a random number, but answered anyway. I swear my heart skipped a beat or two when I answered that phone! There was not a "Hello" the person sounded EXACTALLY like my dad (who had passed away 5 years prior) and answered the phone the same way he always did "Gina?" At first I wasn't sure if it was my dad calling from heaven, if I was dreaming or what was going on. I will never forget that moment, it was very strange! It turns out it was the priest calling to coordinate the Godparents. I got off the phone and texted one of my sisters and told them that dad called me today. I still get chills when I think about that phone call! It was cool and a little creepy (in a good way) at the same time.

Advice

Growing up my parents both had advice of all kinds for us. "Do your best" was what my dad told me every morning. "Never pass up anything free" was one of my dad's comments. I took that to heart one day when I made one of my sisters take home a 4 foot artificial Christmas tree that we got free from a store. She wasn't going to take it, but I made her because my dad always said, "Never pass up anything free." Now it is the big joke in our family that I made her take that tree because my dad said so. I think she still uses it every Christmas now- see I bet you are glad I made you take that tree now!

Christmas

Christmas traditions are another good memory. My mom and dad always wrapped up a pair of socks for each of us. I have no idea where this tradition started or came from, but my sisters and family still do this now when we exchange names for Christmas. Everyone gets a present for the name you picked plus a pair of socks. Socks in general are a good and funny memory for me about my mom. She always had a pair of stripped rainbow socks in her sock drawer that I remember seeing a picture of her wearing those. She always wore decorative socks, but in a subtle way. She would have black or blue dressy socks that had crazy patterns on them and she would wear them with Mary Jane type shoes. So you wouldn't notice unless you looked close. We always joked about my mom's crazy socks, but now I looked in my sock drawer and see that I have a large number of crazy socks myself. I had to laugh when I opened my drawer this morning.

Socks

Another thing we joked about was the compression socks my mom had to wear when she was pregnant with me. There is a picture of her in the middle of summer wearing the tall compression socks because her feet and legs swelled up so big. So when we were cleaning out my mom's room after she passed away my sisters were trying to make me take the compression socks they found. Turns out when I was pregnant my feet swelled up like balloons also, they were kidding around saying it was payback for when my mom was pregnant with me. There were a lot of funny things and in good fun, joking around that happened when we cleaned out our parent's house. Yes, it was sad and we cried and did not want to be there at times, but I look back to that experience and I was able to spend quality time with my sisters and we had a lot of laughs going through our childhood memories.

When we cleaned out my parents' house we saved some of the clothes from my mom that she wore that "looked like mom" and sent them in to have teddy bears created out of the clothes. They all turned out amazing and in our house we call them the Grandma Bears. Now I wished we would have saved some of our dad's clothes to make teddy bears out of too. We did make a quilt for our cabin up north out of all of our dad's flannel shirts. That is basically all he wore, he had one in every color. If you bought him one it had to have exactly nine buttons, if it was 8 buttons it was no good.

Birthday

Laughter is how my family got through a lot of tough and difficult times in our lives. Laughter was also what we did growing up, laughing and having fun. This still happens today, any time my sisters and I get together it is just constant laughing and joking around. I love my family and wouldn't change anything except to have my parents back on this earth, but I know that is not possible and they live with us every day. Just the other day I was thinking about some of the times I remember my dad laughing and one time up north came to mind. I was probably eight years old and my sisters were asking me what we should get our dad for his birthday and what I think he would like.

My response was a toupee... I am pretty sure I had no idea what one was, but I heard some older people talking about toupees once and how they need one. In my simple eight year old mind I thought my dad needed one too! He burst out laughing from the other room! If you knew my dad he basically had a comb over hair cut for many years. In his later years he had a crew cut, as he would call it- basically really short hair or a buzz cut as others would call it. He didn't have many hairs on his head so suggesting a toupee in a serious manner struck his funny bone! Years later he would always joke to me that I thought he needed a toupee. Still makes me giggle now looking back on the situation.

Stinky

This memory about my grandma, my dad's mom, is probably going to get my grandma saying "oh jeeze" in heaven and another person thinking "really?! You had to tell that story". But here goes... So this was one of those memories after a person passes away that you kind of go, "woah!" and think how is that a possible? So I was watching TV in our bedroom while my fiancé was getting his hunting stuff together for a long weekend trip. He closed the door to the master bathroom and came out a few minutes later laughing saying, "I bet you won't miss that smell?" My response was, "Awe, come on at least spray something!" So he found an air freshener from somewhere and all I heard was crrshhhhhhhhhhhheerrrrrrrrrrrrr for about 10 seconds. As soon as I carefully tested the air with one nostril I started laughing.

He asked what was so funny and I said, "That smells exactly like my grandma's old apartment!" still laughing. I went on to tell him that my sisters would take my grandma to the Dollar Store once a month, and she would always have to pick up multiple cans of air fresheners for the bathroom. It was probably because when she sprayed after "going poopy" as she would say, she would hold that spray button down for 10-15 seconds at a time! If you were in her 500 sq. ft. apartment when she had to "go poopy" you would just wait for it... then hear crshhhhhhhhhherrrrrrrrrrrrrrrrrrrrrrrrrrrrrrrrrrrrrrrrrrrrrrrrrrrrrrrrrrrrrrrr and the door open, and then it would hit you... that overpowering air freshener smell. Oh man, I just started laughing after telling him that story, because it was always a funny memory of my grandma. She is probably now shaking her head at me because now the whole world knows, sorry grandma, love you! It is crazy how even a smell can trigger a funny memory of a loved one, but it does I have found that out!

Remembering

So it took me a long time to get to the point of reminiscing about memories with a smile instead of a tear. This morning I was thinking about an upcoming funeral and how people dread going because they are so sad. I challenge you to think about how you would like your own funeral to go? Sounds so morbid and sobering to think that someday that will be you, but it is inevitable. My first thought was oh no I wonder what crazy stories of mine will come out of the woodwork for all to hear, but then I thought, "good". I want people to remember me for the funny and even stupid things I have done in my life to hopefully leave them with joy and happy memories.

I don't want people to be sad over me, yes that is flattering, but why would I want a loved one to go through that grief and pain that I went through with so many loved ones. In a way that helped me realize I shouldn't be focusing on the pity I was having for myself because a loved one was gone, but instead celebrate and smile because of the memories. I now try to think of the good things and happy times I had with each person, remind myself to appreciate the times I have now with everyone who is alive. I take too many pictures, try not to worry about the small stuff, do things I enjoy, live life with a smile and if I do not want to do it, don't- life is too short!

For me the remembering of funny memories was almost therapeutic. Since writing the memories down I find myself thinking about these again with a smile or even a quiet laugh. I have decided this is something I am going to continue to do and I encourage anyone else to do the same. I plan on making a "Laugh Book" for myself to read and remember my loved ones and the smiles they gave me and still give me. At first I thought just written stories, but I know there are some good pictures stored away somewhere that can make that moment come to life again. I think it is important to laugh and think of the joy people in your lives have given you. Remember the joy of the people who have passed, but also give happiness and gratitude to those who are still in your life. Someday those people may not be in your life anymore and you maybe wished you would have thanked them or let them know how much you appreciated them.

Chapter 16

Coincidences and Winks

After my dad passed away I would always see cardinals in random places or see one flying somewhere at the least expected moment. My dad loved cardinals and there was one on my parent's headstone actually. He used to find cardinal Christmas ordainments. They had to always go at the top of the tree, because that is where birds sit, he always told us. So when I would start seeing a cardinal it just reminded me of my dad, and made me think he was near. I then found out that cardinals are supposed to be messages or presence of a passed loved one. In the backyard of our last house there used to be a cardinal that I would see all the time. We went out to eat one day at the golf course and there was a cardinal out there in the middle of the summer. It stayed there the whole entire time we were eating!

I just read this book called, *When God Winks, How the Power of Coincidence Guides Your Life,* by Squire Rushnell. I am not pushing a religion or a belief in God. I personally believe in a higher power and found this book interesting. It explains how coincidences in your life after a loved one passes can bring you comfort or even guidance. When I need it the most I will see a cardinal or hear a Johnny Cash song, and I know that my dad approves or is supporting me. Just as I wrote that, I glanced over at Pinterest and there is a picture of "Winter Birds" it is of three cardinals on a snowy birdhouse... coincidence?!

Quotes

I have always been a quote person and have been collecting quotes in notebooks in grade school and stickers and poster in high school. Now my Pinterest board is filled with 1,600+ quotes that have all spoken to me or moved me in some way. Two people can read the same quote and have two different reactions or emotions towards it. I say if it helps you deal with what you are going through in anyway go with it! If you are looking for more quotes check out my Pinterest page: www.pinterest.com/ginaschampers

Top 10 Quotes

1. You never know how strong you are until being strong is the only choice you have. —Bob Marley
2. Sometimes you will never know the value of a moment until it becomes a memory. – Dr. Seuss
3. Don't die with your music still in you. – Wayne Dyer

4. Enjoy the little things in life for one day you'll look back and realize they were the big things. –Kurt Vonnegut
5. I am thankful for my struggle because without it I wouldn't have stumbled across my strength. –Alexandra Elle
6. You were given this life because you are strong enough to handle it. -Unknown
7. I have learned… life is tough, but I am tougher. -Unknown
8. We don't meet people by accident. They are meant to cross our path for a reason. -Unknown
9. To know even one life has breathed easier because you have lived. This is to have succeeded. –Ralph Waldo Emerson
10. Sometimes the things we cannot change end up changing us. -Unknown

Grief Quotes

Grief isn't something you get over, it's something you go through. – Alan Pedenen

Grief never ends…But it changes. It's a passage, not a place to stay. Grief is not a sign of weakness, nor a lack of faith… It is the price of love. –Unknown

I wasn't prepared for the fact that grief is so unpredictable. It wasn't just sadness, and it wasn't linear. – Meghan O'Rourke

Where there is deep grief, there was deep love. –Zig Ziglar

A family that grieves together heals together. -Unknown

Don't allow others to rush your grief. You have a lifetime to heal and it's a lifelong journey, travel at your own speed! -The Greif Tool Box

Grief changes us, the pain sculpts us into someone who understands more deeply, hurts more often, appreciates more quickly, cries more easily, hopes more desperately, loves more openly. –Unknown.

This is a thing many people outside your grief cannot understand: that you have not simply lost one person, at one point in time. You have lost their presence in every aspect of your life. Your future has changed as well as your "now." -Megan Devine

Moving on doesn't meant that you forget about things. It just means you have to accept what happened and continue living. -Unknown

We do not heal the past by dwelling there; we heal the past by living fully in the present. -Marianne Williamson

Sometimes your heart needs more time to accept what your mind already knows. -Unknown

Sometimes, life is just hard, and some days are just rough... and sometimes you just gotta cry before you can move forward... (and all of that is ok). -Unknown

It takes a strong soul with real heart to develop smiles out of situations that make us weep. -Unknown

Time won't make you forget, it'll make you grow and understand things. -Unknown

Challenges

We don't grow when things are easy; we grow when we face challenges. –Joyce Meyer

She stood in the storm, and when the wind did not blow her way, she adjusted her sails. –Elizabeth Edwards

When you come out of the storm you won't be the same person that walked in. That's what the storm is all about. -Haruki Murakami

And once the store is over you won't remember how you made it through, how you managed to survive. You won't even be sure, in fact, whether the storm is really over. But one this is certain. When you come out of the storm you won't be the same person who walked in. –Haruki Murakami

Healing comes when we choose to walk away from darkness and move towards a brighter light. – Dieter F. Uchtdof

She was drowning, but nobody saw her struggle. -Unknown

Remember how far you have come, not just how far you have to go. You are not where you want to be, but neither are you where you used to be. –Rick Warren

Life's challenges are not supposed to paralyze you, they're supposed to help you discover who you are. –Bernice Johnson Reagon

Be strong because things will get better. It may be stormy now, but it never rains forever. -Arashi

There are plenty of obstacles in your path. Don't allow yourself to become one of them. –Ralph Marston

When something bad happens you have three choices. You can either let it define you. Let it destroy you, or you can let it strengthen you. -Unknown

There are moments which mark your life. Moments when you realize nothing will ever be the same and time is divided into two parts- before this, and after this. –Fallen

You've seen my decent. Now watch me rising. -Rumi

When Someone Has Passed

It's hard to forget someone; who gave you so much to remember. -Unknown

Perhaps they are not stars in the sky, but rather openings where our loved ones shine down to let us know they are happy. –Eskimo Proverb

Those we love don't go away. They walk beside us every day… unseen, unheard, but always near, still loved, still missed and very dear. -Unknown

Feathers appear when Angels are near. -Unknown

I don't think you will fully understand how you've touched my life. I don't think you could know how special you are, that even on my darkest nights you are my brightest star. –Erica Jong

Death leaves heartache no one can heal, love leaves a memory no one can steal. –From a headstone in Ireland

I never got to say goodbye. Wish I could go back to the day when angels came and took you away. I wanted to hold your hand so tight, kiss you gently and say good night. And then just before you had to go I would tell you how much 'I love you so'. I don't know how I don't know why I never got the change to say goodbye. —John F Connor

Grandmothers create memories that the heart holds forever. -Unknown

My father gave me the greatest gift anyone could give another person, he believed in me. – Jim Valvano

Words can't wipe away your tears. Hugs won't ease your pain. But hold on to your memories, forever they'll remain. -Unknown

There are moments in life when you miss someone so much that you just want to pick them from your dreams and hug them for real.- Charlie Brown

Goodbyes are not forever. Goodbyes are not the end. They simply mean I'll miss you, until we meet again. -Unknown

Crying isn't a sign of weakness. It's a sign of having tried too hard to be strong for too long. -Unknown

Family isn't always blood. It's the people in your life who want you in heirs; the ones who accept you for who you are. The ones who would do anything to see your smile and who love you no matter what. —Unknown

It is not the length of life, but the depth - Ralph Waldo Emerson.

Change

Everybody has gone through something that has changed them in a way that they could never go back to the person they once were. -Unknown

Life is too short for the "have-to's" to hardly make time for the "want-to's" –Tal Ben Shahar, Ph. D

Getting knocked down in life is a given. Getting up and moving forward is a choice. –Zig Ziglar

Take all the time you need to heal emotionally. Moving on doesn't take a day. It takes a lot of little steps to be able to break free of your broken self. –Tere Arigo

Strength shows, not only in the ability to persist, but the ability to start over. F. Scott Fitzgerald

I may not be there yet. But I am closer than I was yesterday. One step can make all the difference. -Unknown

Life has knocked me down a few times. It has shown me things I never wanted to see. I have experienced sadness and failures. But one this is for sure… I always get up! –Unknown

New beginnings are often disguised as painful endings…" –Lao Tzu

You can't change what's going on around you until you start changing what's going on within you. –Zig Ziglar

Don't confuse your path with your destination. Just because it's stormy now doesn't mean that you aren't headed for sunshine. –Unknown

Where you are now is not where you will always be… There are brighter days up ahead. –Joel Osteen

One of the happiest moments in life is when you find the courage to let go of what you can't change. -Unknown

Most humans are never fully present in the now, because unconsciously they believe that the next moment must be more important than this one. But then you miss your whole life, which is never not now. And that's a revelation for some people: to realize that your life is only ever now. –Eckhart Tolle.

Every single thing that has ever happened in your life is preparing you for a moment that is yet to come. -Unknown

Recommended Reading

Awakening Your Life's Purpose, by Eckhart Tolle

Happier, by Tal Ben Shahar

I Can See Clearly Now, by Wayne Dyer

The Magic, by Rhonda Byrne

The Power, by Rhonda Byrne

The Secret, by Rhonda Byrne

The Shift, by Wayne Dyer

The Unmistakable Touch of Grace, by Cheryl Richardson

You Can Heal Your Life, by Louise Hayes

When God Winks, How the Power of Coincidence Guides Your Life, by Squire Rushnell

Notes/Memories:

I encourage you to think back of the fun memories of the loved ones who have passed. Start your own "Laugh Book" to reference when you need a smile or want to think about that person or persons in a happy way.

Printed in the United States
By Bookmasters